© Copyright 2021 - All rights reserved.

You may not reproduce, duplicate or send the contents of this book without direct written permission from the author. You cannot hereby despite any circumstance blame the publisher or hold him or her to legal responsibility for any reparation, compensations, or monetary forfeiture owing to the information included herein, either in a direct or an indirect way.

Legal Notice: This book has copyright protection. You can use the book for personal purpose. You should not sell, use, alter, distribute, quote, take excerpts or paraphrase in part or whole the material contained in this book without obtaining the permission of the author first.

Disclaimer Notice: You must take note that the information in this document is for casual reading and entertainment purposes only. We have made every attempt to provide accurate, up to date and reliable information. We do not express or imply guarantees of any kind. The persons who read admit that the writer is not occupied in giving legal, financial, medical or other advice. We put this book content by sourcing various places.

Please consult a licensed professional before you try any techniques shown in this book. By going through this document, the book lover comes to an agreement that under no situation is the author accountable for any forfeiture, direct or indirect, which they may incur because of the use of material contained in this document, including, but not limited to, — errors, omissions, or inaccuracies.

WELCOME TO THE OCEAN

OCEAN

An Ocean is a very huge body covered of salt water. It presents 70% of Earth's surface. There is only one world ocean, it is divided into five main areas with no borders. Smaller parts of the ocean are called seas.

PACIFIC

Pacific Ocean is the largest of Earth's oceans. Its surface is more than all the dry lands together. It is bounded by the continents of Asia and Australia in the west and the Americas in the east.

ATLANTIC

Atlantic Ocean is the second largest of Earth's oceans. Most of Earth rivers water flow into the Atlantic. Its S-shaped basin extending longitudinally between Europe and Africa to the east, and the Americas to the west

INDIAN

Indian Ocean is the third largest of Earth's oceans. It was sailed by traders to exchange goods between India, Africa, and Arabia. It is bounded by Asia to the north, Africa to the west and Australia to the east

ARCTIC

Arctic Ocean is the world smallest and shallowest ocean. It is also known by being the coldest. than all the dry lands together. It occupies the most northern region of Earth.

SOUTHERN

The Southern Ocean is also known as the Antarctic Ocean because it surrounds Antarctica.

OCEAN MOST WONDERFUL ANIMALS

OCTOPUS

I have three hearts.
I have very good eyesight and
an excellent sense of touch.
I am invertebrate,
which means I have no backbones.

DOLPHIN

I am a marine mammal.
I breathe through a blowhole on the top of my head.
I am carnivore, I eat mostly fish and squid. I m the most intelligent animal in the ocean.

My Name Is CRAB

CRAB

I am decapod, which means I am ten-footed. I live in all the world's oceans, in fresh water, and on land. There are over 4500 species of me.

SHARK

I don't have any bone in my body.
I live for about 25 years.
You might know me as human-killer but I only attack if I am scared.

My Name Is WHALE

WHALE

I am the largest animal on Earth and I live in every ocean. I am a mammal, which means I nurse my babies. The blue whale is the largest animal on Earth; can weigh more than 200 tons and stretch up to 100 feet long.

I produce otherworldly vocalizations that can be heard for miles underwater.

STARFISH

I can only live in warm water.
I am invertebrate too.
I have five arms.
Unlike you, I don't have blood.

SEA TURTLE

I can hold my breath for 30 minutes. I can't live on the Arctic Ocean because it's too cold there. eat all kinds of food including sea grass, seaweed, crabs, jellyfish, and shrimp

SEAL

I am carnivorous mammal.
I usually feeds on fish,
squid, shellfish, crustaceans
or sea birds.
i can sleep underwater.

JELLYFISH

I have been in the ocean for millions of years, before dinosaurs lived on the Earth. I live in cold and warm ocean water, deep water and along coastlines. Despite my name, I'm not actually a fish—I am invertebrate, which means I have no backbones. I have tiny stinging cells in my tentacles to stun or paralyze the prey. Inside my bell-shaped body is an opening that is my mouth.

SEA HORSE

I am a tiny fis. They call me Sea horse cause my head looks like a tiny horse.
I am carnivore too.

STINGRAY

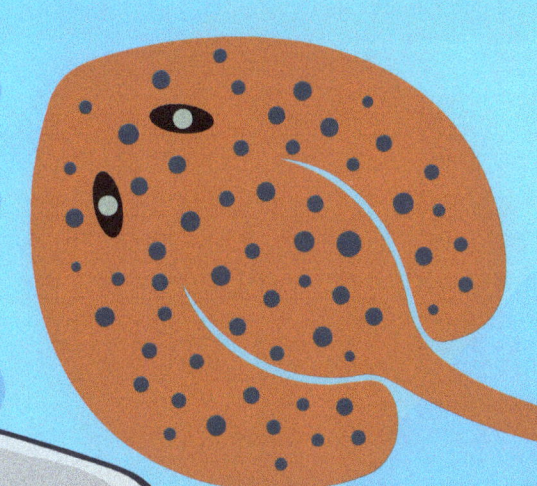

I live in tropical and subtropical coastal ocean waters.

I have venomous stingers on my tail which I only use in self-defence.

Like my cousin, the shark, I do not have bones. My flat body allows me to dig in and hide from predators on the sandy ocean bottom.

My eyes are on top of my body and my mouth, gills, and nostrils are on the underside. I can't see my pray, but I use smell to find food. I eat molluscs, crabs, clams, oysters, sea snails and small fish.

OYSTER

I am edible. I like to eat algae, which is a type of plant material that lives in the water.
I have shells that are usually shaped like ovals or pears

My

Name

Is

CORAL

CORAL

I am in fact animal, not plant. Together with my friends, I create coral reefs, which are the largest biological structures on Earth. Coral reefs are naturally colorful because of algae, which lives inside of the coral. I protect the wildlife and clean the ocean. Please protect me by using less water and be kind to nature, because it helps, you, humans live on this beautiful planet Earth.

- You can find mountains and volcanoes on the bottom of oceans. The world's longest mountain chain is underwater.
- The deepest point in the ocean is the Mariana Trench.

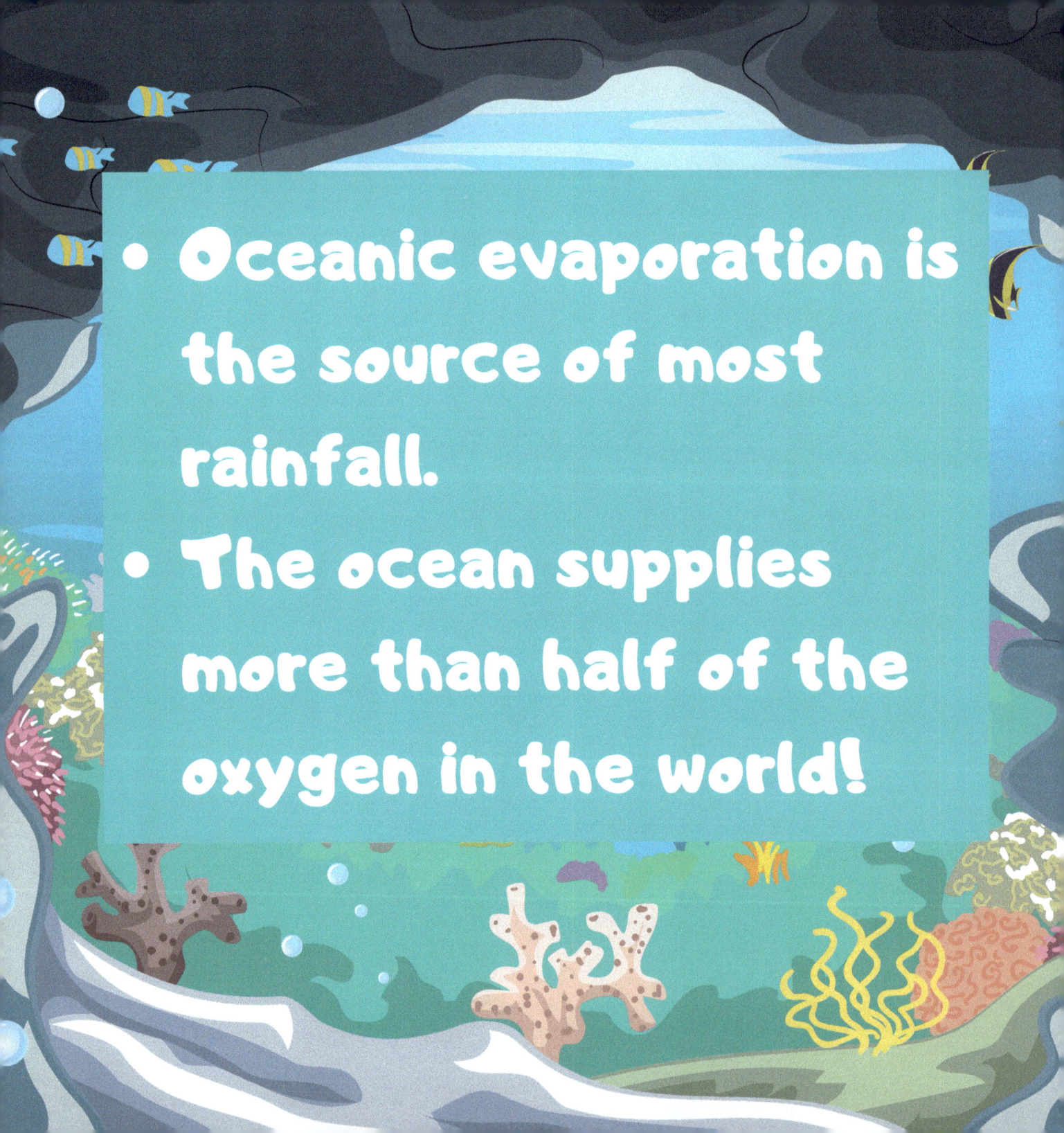
- Oceanic evaporation is the source of most rainfall.
- The ocean supplies more than half of the oxygen in the world!

Thank you!

We hope you enjoyed our book.

As a small family company, your feedback is very important to us.

Please let us know how you like our book through a review on amazon and at:

wallstersbookshelf@gmail.com

 Wallster's Book Shelf

 @wallstersbookshelf

www.ingramcontent.com/pod-product-compliance
Lightning Source LLC
LaVergne TN
LVHW070222080526
838202LV00068B/6883